WORDS OF A GOAT PRINCESS

Jessie Reyez

Andrews McMeel
PUBLISHING®

Andrews McMeel Publishing
a division of Andrews McMeel Universal
1130 Walnut Street, Kansas City, Missouri 64106

www.andrewsmcmeel.com

24 25 26 27 28 MCN 10 9 8 7 6 5 4 3 2

ISBN: 978-1-5248-9029-2

Library of Congress Control Number: 2023941395

Editor: Danys Mares
Art Director: Holly Swayne
Production Editor: Dave Shaw
Production Manager: Alex Alfano

ATTENTION: SCHOOLS AND BUSINESSES
Andrews McMeel books are available at quantity discounts with bulk purchase for educational, business, or sales promotional use. For information, please e-mail the Andrews McMeel Publishing Special Sales Department: sales@amuniversal.com.

Dedicated to my motherfucking self

CONTENTS

INTRODUCTION

Life is just a series of ups and downs
Like the chest of a loved one while they sleep
Like the ridges and summits we cling to on the screen of a heart
    monitor
Where the advent of the flat line haunts us
And yet
We spend life chasing equilibrium
Chasing a higher frequency
Where the peaks and valleys aren't as intense
Chasing Zen
Chasing peace
Chasing the flat line of the horizon
When in the end
The only thing we can really depend on
is knowing
that we are all heading there inevitably
To the flat line
To the fields of Eden
To peace
But before peace—

there is chaos

1

PORTALS

Every now and then I get a window amidst the hate
Whenever I see an old crumb that old love left behind
It acts like a tiny portal
Like the Lollapalooza sticker you gave me that I forgot to rip off my
    guitar case
And in those moments
In between the palpable disdain I have for you
As if in between an inhale and an exhale
I get a small peephole of nostalgia
And like the Big Bang
A little universe is born
And in that moment
I wish I could kiss every metaphorical bruise I ever gave you
In that moment
I take full responsibility and forget ever needing an apology from
    you
In that moment
I wish I could get back every night we ever wasted
And I wish I could take back every fight
And every *I hate you*
That I didn't mean
But then time runs out
And the exhale drops
And the heartbeat of my disdain returns
And I feel as though a ghost has walked through the room

2

TOPANGA CANYON

I'm standing at the edge looking down at the car wreck
The rented Lexus we got is crushed at the foot of this cliff
Topanga Canyon said today's the day I guess
Smoke fills the air
I look to my right and my jaw drops when I see my body on the
    ground
And in this moment
I realize I'm spirit now
I am dead
If I were carnal
I would've fainted at this point
But I am not
I am the is-ness now
My emotions teeter
I am the is-ness now
Finally
I come back to the moment
I watch thick blood slowly escape from my cracked skull onto the
    gray pavement
And I wonder why I listened to you when you said "Faster!"
I look for you
For your body
Then for your spirit
But find nothing
Then I remember
You weren't in the car
But I was drinking
And thinking
of you
Drinking and thinking of you

That's what resentment does
It makes you think
that the poison you drink
will kill them

3
A GOWN

I walk around town with people knowing what you did
I wear it
Like a bright pink obnoxious gown
A dress with tulle so coarse it makes my skin bleed
But I wear it anyway
I wear it
Around anyone that knows our history
Around your friends
Around my family
Everywhere
The dress has a corsette that squeezes the air out of my lungs
And treats me like a rag getting rinsed of its last drop before it's dry
But I smile anyway
As if it's my duty to wear it
Because I chose to wear it didn't I?
I walk around and feel their eyes say
"That's the girl that chose to stay after he cheated"
And I do it
I wear it
Publicly
Like a sex toy billboard in a Christian neighborhood
Like a cow getting butchered in India
Like a piercing siren to a deaf crowd
So loud
So dismal
And yet
So inutile
A clown in a gown

4

WOODS

If I did
I would admit it
but I don't miss a thing anymore
Now there's just trust issues I can't shake
And they ruin new love
And they ruin sunny days
But not like clouds do
They ruin sunny days like a death in the family
Bleak
Your memories make my healing drag its feet
And I'm tired
I think I'm ready to cut my ankles off if that's what it takes to be
    free
I'd rather bleed out and smile my last seconds away
Than suffer you another moment
My beautiful destruction is over
The season has passed
Mother Nature has spoken
It's time to set fire to the dry woods

5
SURPRISE

Surprise
I'm still not over my ex yet
But I saved a bit of pride being the first one to exit
Surprise
I got a few white hairs in
But I haven't felt the urge to fertilize my eggs yet
Watching red-eyed dead tired parents makes me feel like it's a
    blessing to be intentionally barren
Is it really that bad to grow old alone?
Is it really that scary?
Marriage seems overrated
Marriage seems like good sex eradicated
Fun incarcerated
Divorce rates are inflating, no?
As beautiful a union young lovebirds may make
And as high as they may fly
Winds can change
And wings can break
Everyone has dark secrets they've never told their wives
Or their husbands
And secrets come out inevitably
And most people will hate each other eventually
Most people play fast and loose with the truth
A white lie borrowed and something blue
Up until you die of course
That's when everything changes
And everything you've ever done wrong
is forgiven
by those still tied to earth
Because everyone loves the dead
I've seen a miserable wife turn into the most devastated widow
Because absence makes the heart grow . . . stupid

Maybe my soulmate's dead
"So many fish in the sea"
Schools of fish?
Because I fucking hated school
And institutions did nothing for me but try to dull my color
So I'm apprehensive of an institutionalized lover
And now
Although my younger days are in the clouds
When I'm sixty
And look back to now
These days I'm in
will be my younger days
And when my head is fully gray
And I hear them say
"She would've been a beautiful bride"
I'll smile
Cause yeah fucking right
There's a really good chance
that I'm going to die a child

6
JAM

He was a jar of strawberry jam that was stuck
I put in the work and sweat
I ripped my fingernails from their beds
while the friction from beneath my grip gave way
I cried
I lost sleep
I tried
Everything
And got nothing but a budge
My passion was the arm that barely loosened him
And when I needed a moment to breathe
To fight heart atrophy
To regain strength
She came along
Opened the fridge
Grabbed the jar
Blew a kiss
And the top flew off

7
LEFT OUT

When I was five
I remember wondering
"What does everyone else see when they close their eyes?"
I remember asking a classmate and seeing a glazed gaze look back
   at me
Mute
I remember walking home
I remember the day ending
I remember being frightened of the dark
And sneaking into my parents' room at night
Where I would lay my blanket on the floor by my dad's side of the
   bed
I remember asking my father the same question
"Que ves cuando cerrás los ojos?"
"Oscuridad" he answered
"Darkness"
Black
It left me perplexed
If I was so scared of the dark
How come I was never scared of the abyss on the other side of my
   eyelids
He fell asleep
I closed my eyes
I remember seeing a billion stars at once
I remember wondering if they were looking back at me
Thinking to themselves that they had fucked up
And put a weathered soul in a little body
by accident
In the wrong system
On the wrong rock
Where she would forever feel out of place
Asking people questions
that no one would ever have the real answers to

8
IDENTITY

"Don't you miss me" says the dark
"Thought we were friends" says my art
"Who was there for you?
When you couldn't eat?
When you couldn't sleep?
When love wouldn't let your heart beat
who gave it music?
It was me!
It was me!"

A slow-moving gentle giant
with sky blue skin
stands over my muse's dying body
my point of view jumps back and forth from both sets of eyes
like a fruitless sport
I am healing
Then I am the dark
Then I am the healing
Then I am the dark

Suddenly the world freezes
And it dawns on me
I've been scared of mental stability
The same way man fears the unknown
And I've been drunk dancing with mental fragility
Who's gripping me close
And whispering that it wants to take me home
Again
So it can bend me over like it always has
So it can watch me paint after we've done the deed
Because my colors always look so much more vibrant after I've been
    fucked
And it makes me question myself

If I blossomed in the dark
Am I really all that I can be when I'm happy?
Am I really me when I'm happy?

9
SAD DRUNK HONEY EYES

She was just fifteen when first love came
And her innocence evaporated
like a raindrop in July
The first time he brought her to her peak
Neon rainbows were born in her mind's eye
Naivety made her smile when she found herself at the mercy of first
    love
Until it too evaporated
And left her mouth full of sand
And left her skin dry
And left her mirror full of self-hatred
She'd leave her class to cry in the bathroom
He'd already replaced her
She'd go home to cry in her bathroom
And pray for salvation
And in sad whispers
The bathroom walls would echo her voice back to her
"Why didn't anyone tell me love makes you want to die"
"Why didn't anyone tell me love makes you want to die"
She would steal liquor from her father's collection
Sometimes Guaro
Sometimes white rum
Anything to get the job done
She would fill the empty bottles up with water
And try her hardest to hide her darkness from parents
But her mother knew
She knew unrequited love
lived in the heavy blue bags
under her daughter's
sad
drunk
honey
eyes

10
WASTE

I don't want to risk you hating me
So I'd rather keep you at bay
Because you ignore the ten-foot waves of my emotions
And you think that you can save me
But your sweet green gaze doesn't see
Although I am drowning
I am also the ocean

You think you can nurse me back to love
But an amputation is what I actually need
And I always turn the doctor away
Sometimes I feel like the past is who I am
And like I'd rather limp than lose it completely

"Your heart is big enough to fit me in there" you say
But it's me AND my bullshit
And my baggage doesn't fit in a stadium
It doesn't fit in dreams fulfilled
So how could your arms ever embrace that which refuses to hold
    itself?

I hate that I found love while being so broken
You pour it into me
Profusely
But it just leaks out of me
My love
You are the feast that my mother's prayers prepared for me
But I keep ungratefully screaming that I am full
My love
You are like eleven pounds of L.A. weed without a lighter in sight

What a waste of a good man
To have found me drowning
To have built me a lifeboat
To have thrown me a life jacket
Just to watch me turn around
And swim deeper into the water

11
ONCE

I went through your phone twenty times
But I only told you once
I knew exactly what you had done
And when you had done it
But had I told you
what I had found
You would've turned it all around
And you would've told me that I broke YOUR trust again
And I would have said "I'm sorry"
I'm sorry
For
Your
Fuckery
Because that's what you would always do
Drug my gravity
Slingshot my tears back at me
And make me apologize
For your mistakes
I don't know why I used my phone to take photos of the photos
    I found
Photos of the evidence
Because I still chose to bite my tongue anyway
And ignore the taste of blood
And still stand by your side
Now next to you
I feel pathetic
until I remember
One of the texts I found
that felt like a gift
One of the texts I read
had you getting curbed by another woman
And I laugh
And I get to soothe my ego for a split second

And bask in the rejection that you suffered from another
And find relief and revel in someone deeming you unworthy
But then the anesthesia wears off
And I remember that's what you do to me
And the bubble bursts
And the tears are let loose again
Tears that blur my vision
And I don't wipe them away
And I choose to be blind
And I cry
I cry without telling you why

12
BILLBOARD

Being born a woman
is being born walking uphill
So instead I dance a waltz
up every mountain I climb

Being born a woman
is being scared to be too proud
So instead I smile with my head high and say thank you
as if the accolades have been longing to be home

Being born a woman
is delicately tiptoeing around the egos in the room
So instead I sit boldly in my purpose
because I am the perfect fit

Being born a woman
is feeling a convoluted mix of gratitude and fear if she's the only
    woman at the table
So instead I honor the sisters before me
and burn down doors just to let my younger sisters in

Being born a woman
is being told to wear a bra to keep the pious public comfortable
So instead I honor my breasts with the freedom of a thin white
    t-shirt
at church

I dance barefoot up the snow-covered summit

Just to smile in the face of the oppressor

And when my audacity triggers the blood into his cheeks

I wink

For I know men are afraid of women

Who are not afraid of them

13
PEACE

I am not breathing
That's just the trees taking what is owed to them
I am not dancing
That's just the wind taking over my limbs
I am not crying
That's just the rain falling on my face
I am not angry
That's just the eternal flame being fanned by the winds of untamed
    emotions within my heart
I am not standing
That's just my soul rooting down through the soft blades of green
    grass
I am not smiling
That's just the sun caressing my face from the inside of my soul
I am not peace
That's just the oneness and its recognition
I am not aging
That's just time painting beautiful thin pathways of memories on my
    skin
And I am not dying
That's just my spirit going home

14
DIABLA

Ya no me molesta cuando me decís diabla
Ya aprendí a reírme y abrazar esos prejuicios
está bien
dígame diabla
Pero lo que no sabes
Es que a mí me lucen mis cuernos
Como si fueran una corona
Y yo sé que te mata
Verme enamorada
con la reflexión mía
que tanto odias
Y yo sé que te mata
Saber que tus palabras no me llegan como puñaladas
Pero como flores a mis pies

15
GOOD

What good are my words if we don't speak the same language?
What good is my voice if your eardrums have ruptured?
What good are these love songs to you then?
What good is my kiss if your skin longs for another woman?
What good is my touch if you wince?
What good is patience if the time has run out?
What good is a doctor if the blood runs cold?
What good is a nun to the devil?

No I am not the nun

No I am not the devil

And no

I am of no good to you

16
STILL

In a silent room
You can still hear music when you think of a song
Is that magic or a curse?
Or worse?
I guess it's contingent on the song

I can still feel you in an empty room

17
PELADA

Pelada
¿Por qué lloras por un hombre
que no te valora?
Diosito no te dio lágrimas para estar llorando todos los días
Hermana
Yo que haría
Yo que daría
para abrirte esos ojitos aguados

Pelada
Cuando te veo
Me veo a mí
Hace años yo también estaba así
Perdonando lo imperdonable
Y olvidando lo inolvidable
"Es hombre y ellos son así"
son consejos brutos

Pelada
El hombre que yo amaba
Escondía su celular
Con la clave re larga
Era super defensivo
Y habían muchos signos que yo ignoraba
Y me hacía la ciega
Por querer ser ciega
Por quererlo a él

Pelada
El hombre fiel es un libro abierto
Hermana
no gaste su tiempo
Esa relación nació muerta
¿Por qué sigues buscando agua fresca en un desierto?
¿Por qué sigues esperando el calorcito en pleno invierno?

Pelada
Te va dejar pelada

18
WOULD'VE

You would've never been a good dad
You would've complained about the kids wanting to sleep in our bed
You would've dropped them off at school before work
And never looked back
to make sure that they felt loved
and cared for
that extra little bit
Instead they would've watched you drive off to your true love

You would've made me beg for a date night after weeks of neglect
You would've drank too much at dinner and then yelled at me for
    noticing
You would've made the babysitter feel uncomfortable when we got
    home
She would've been too worried to mention it to me
but I would've seen it in her face

You would've turned the volume up anytime you would've heard me
    crying in the bathroom
You would've made our daughter question my judgment for having
    stayed with you
You would've made our daughter pay for your karma
You would've denied any blame
And remained allergic to onus
But you would've cringed
every time you'd have to watch her cry
over boys just like you

You would've left me after your second million
And you will leave your second wife after your third
Until you are as wrinkled as a raisin
Because men like you will never be happy
Perennially empty
Always thirsty
Your cup will never be full
Even in a flood
And so the raisin will continue to wither
And the stone will sink
But at least you'll die with your pockets full

19
BITCH

She does not wear tight clothes
when she is out alone
She wears her t-shirt
like it's armor
She hates being told she's pretty
Because she knows
If she does not respond
She will be called a bitch
She walks by a group of men
And looks at the pavement
And fakes a phone call
As an attempt to escape the inevitable
They yell
"slow down"
She walks a little faster
Her spine tenses
"Bitch"
She ignores them
"Why don't you smile more?!"
She is scared to smile
when she is out alone
Because they think it's an invitation
To be pursued
Even though she just wants to make it home
So she lowers her gaze to the pavement
Speeds up her pace
Locks indifference into her face
And lets them call her a bitch
All in the name
Of hoping to make it home
Safe

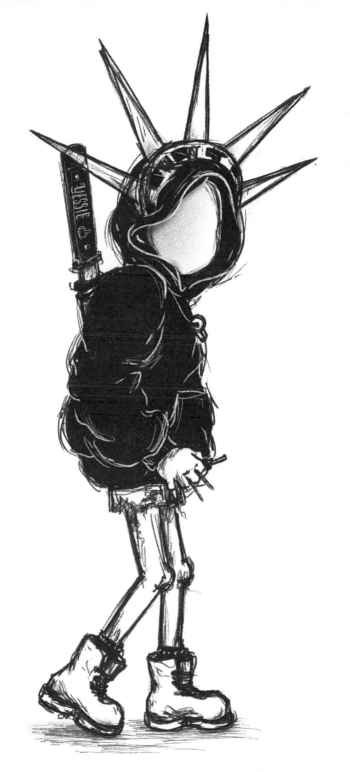

20
GHOST

I once met a lady in her fifties
I'm still not sure what made her feel so comfortable
But she chose me to confide in
She told me that every ten years
she would still meet with her teenage love
who had married someone else
She had never told a soul this secret
Then the strangest smile
crept onto her face
When she spoke of how they would try to pacify their mistakes
in stolen moments
Hotel rooms
Late nights
She said that in their youth
They were poison together
But old age teaches one how to put a sock in the mouth of pride
And muffle its bullshit
Old age teaches you that sometimes being right
isn't worth the fight
Well
I'm still young
And her story haunts me
Because I think of what I let go
When I was just trying to spare us both the pain
Because combined
we are cyanide
And it turns out
That I prefer a peaceful life
But some nights
I am terrified
That in ten years' time
I'll be the one trying to pacify
Our reluctant goodbye

So I've been reading self-help books
And I've accepted that I'm a mess
And anytime I miss your lips
I bite my tongue instead
I hold in every regret
I delete every draft text
I throw my phone in the other room if I'm drinking
Even when I want you close
Because I decided long ago
That I didn't want to watch us die slow
Corazón
I learned I really loved you
the day I let you go

21
FOOTPRINTS

You left your footprints on my chest
It's funny
How every time I think of you
I feel the weight of you press down on my lungs
And a lump manifests in my throat
Because the emotion has nowhere to go
But I refuse to cry
So I force a smile instead
And the rebellion of my body
against my heart
creates a war
that crushes anything I feel
that's not in alignment
with the expression on my face
So the tears that are locked inside compress
And compress
And compress
And the emotion and the hatred pack into each other
without room for even an atom
Suddenly
They turn into diamonds
And I am covered in the jewels of heartbreak
"That's the girl who wears pain like it's gold"
And I smile
Affably
I feel their pity clothe me
Because they think it is a lunatic's agony masked in fantasy
When the real fantasy was ever thinking your love was real
And the reality
Is the alchemy
that left me with diamonds encrusted into my pain
And songs on my guitar
And poems in my notebook
And accolades on my shelf
And footprints on my chest

22
HAPPILY

I wear my sadness on the surface
Because the years have taught me that nothing is perfect
Perfection is pure fiction
Perfect love is a lie we tell children
And those stories die when the movie's over
Everyone misses somebody
Everyone has their own burdens
Even the most perfect people have red flags
hidden in a box beneath their bed
And although it's the human condition to fake it
until the smile feels a little less like makeup
Getting hurt is fated
Problems in a relationship
are as inescapable
as not getting wet
in the middle of the Pacific
so I'd rather cry in the arms of broken love
Because making up
is my favorite kind of makeup
I don't need a healthy relationship
I don't need a diamond ring
I don't need a white gown
Because wedding dresses stain
I'd rather take your bad days
Happily
(ever after)

23

M-SECTION

I was sixteen
We would drink copious amounts of Jose Cuervo in her basement
I would hold her hair back when she needed to throw up
She would blast Kendrick Lamar
every time her parents would let us take the car
We would drive down Bathurst Street
And belly laugh about everything and anything
Even the unfunny
Our nieces would have playdates
We would pretend to be moms together
Practicing
Because it was obvious we would be there for each other in old age
She made it safe for me to be a weirdo
Her family was mine
And mine was hers
When her dad found out I didn't want to go to my graduation
Because I was always talking about how much I hated school
And I didn't want to pay for the gown
He was shocked at my indifference
and insisted that he pay
I remember saying
"Thank you but no
School is not for me
Music is
And I'll be famous one day"
Big impossible dreams
But she would agree with me
She used to listen to my shitty little love songs and cheer
And when my shyness would make me shrink
She'd ask to hear them again

We both lived around the m-section
MacKay Street
Maitland Street
Majestic Crescent
I would often ride my bike to her house
Even at 1:00 a.m.
If I needed to cry about a boy
A boy who had long moved on without me
And when the darkest sentences would stumble out of my mouth
She would listen
She knew about me wrestling with suicide
She knew about how I guzzled my dad's aguardiente
She knew I'd refill those empty bottles with lies from the faucet
to hide my six-foot fathom depressions
She knew of the battles I was losing
She knew where all my bodies were buried
So when I found out that my secrets had never been safe in her
heart
And when I found out that I had been lied to again and again
and again
Over the span of seven formative years
And when I found out that I was being used as a tool
As a Facebook bait and switch mule
For the sake of getting the men she couldn't get on her own
And when I found out the person I trusted more than my own
shadow
was wearing a mask the whole time I loved her
I crumbled
I would've died for her
So that betrayal broke me
more than she will ever know
And in the ruins she left behind
I vowed to never open my heart to a girl like that again

Not the way I had with her at least

Breaking up with a boy hurts a bit

But breaking up with your best friend

Is a different kind of pain

Because you become each other over the years

You share the same coming-of-age memories
You share losing your virginity
You share fearing the daunting reality of post–high school life
You share drunk embarrassments and you share the hangovers
You share nerves while holding hands over the precipice of doing
    drugs for the first time
You share the same words
And you share the same jokes
So when you're forced to say goodbye
You never see that part of you again
And yet
you still see them every day in yourself

Sometimes when I laugh
I still hear her

24
BUNNY

I remember the first time you said you loved me
It was the middle of July
in Miami
The music was too loud
The smoke was too thick
The lasers were too bright
We were about ten-men deep
And you were about ten shots in
We had all lost and found each other by the DJ booth
In an effort to not lose your friends again
I grabbed you with my right hand
And one of your boys with my left
When we got to an opening in the ocean of people
I noticed your demeanor had changed
I asked you if you were okay
and you gave me a short "yes"
I suggested that we go outside and get some air
So we did
And there was my first taste of the real you
Your tongue stung me with such ease
I asked you to calm down
And tell me why you were so furious
But you wouldn't
I was three shots in and twenty-one years old

So immaturity took hold
And I got mad at you for being mad at me
Which just added fuel to the fire
But in your incensed anger you finally screamed the truth at me
"Why the fuck were you grabbing Bunny's hand?! You think I didn't
    see that?!"
Followed by a look that I had never seen you give me before
A look that had a dash of jealousy and a sporadic flash of vitriol
Drunk vitriol
I fiercely defended myself
And so began our first big drunk fight
I called you an idiot for not seeing the obvious
I was just trying to help
And only grabbed your friend's hand
In an effort to "not lose everyone in the club again," I repeated
Then
In the middle of this war of words
In the middle of the screams
You grabbed my hand
Pulled me in
And with mixed emotions
You yelled
"Don't you know I love you?!"
And then silence
And the world paused for a second

And I felt special
From the pavement to the moon
With three simple words
How stupid
How stupid of me to remember the first time you said "I love you"
Because when I brought it up the next day
you looked puzzled
I recounted again, disheartened
And only then did you vaguely recall it
Or feigned to at least
But when I brought it up years later
you told me it never happened
That night should have been the first red flag
You had shown me what I was in for
You had shown me a glimpse of truth
A peek through the window
Into the shack
That I thought was a kingdom
Your kingdom
All hail the addiction king
Cheers to smoking and drinking and women and public validation
Forever competing with other men
Even when they're not competing with you
And when you win
You just want another battle

And another trophy
Forever hungry
Never at peace
And yet
I loved you regardless

25
REBELS

Marriage is Disney incarnate
Divorces are documentaries
Regret is buried with the dearly departed
And truth and society are enemies
If you see me in a white dress
send help
I don't want to give my life away and be a wife
But in the event that the world's orbit reverses
And in the event that I do marry
He will be a feminist
And if I have children
They will be rebels
And if they go to school
They will question teachers
And if my children have children
Their children will be rebels too

26
PINK SKIES

I remember working all night
Wearing painful high-heeled shoes and double-padded push-up
    bras
In that fertile Florida heat
I remember having to muscle a smile when men's eyes would lock
on to my tits
because I knew it meant they'd probably leave the tab open
I remember begging the DJ to play my demos
And I remember getting brushed off
I remember 4:00 a.m. last call being a lie
I remember drunks slowly trickling out of the club at 5:30 a.m.
I remember my manager telling me I would be something one day
I remember being good friends with one of the other bartenders
I had come to love her actually
She was like a big sister
I remember her teaching me how to make Long Island iced teas
    with two bottles in each hand at a time
so I could make them faster
And so I could make as much tips as her to add to our pool
I learned quickly
And the money came quicker
And soon my pile became bigger than hers
I remember counting our tips on the rooftop
Right before the sun would rise
While the sky was still pink
I remember turning over my silver bucket twice one night and
    anxiously saying
"I'm missing a bill"
And she got angry at me
Because she thought I was penny-pinching our pool and tripping
    over one dollar
She didn't know that for a Toronto girl,
"I'm missing a bill"

is slang for
"I'm missing a hundred dollars"
I remember recounting desperately to make sure I had just made a
  mistake
And it *was* just a mistake
Thankfully
But she was already drunk and attitude heavy
And naively I didn't know why
The sun made its way higher into the sky that Sunday morning
The entire staff and I walked over to the bar that was still open
  across the road
like we always did
I remember the busboy whispering "She's pissed at you"
I remember being confused for a moment and asking her to talk
I told her it wasn't what she thought
But she turned her back to me
Swiftly
And just like that
We weren't cool anymore
We didn't speak anymore
We just worked around the tension
For days
Then weeks
But I still had hope for an eventual reconciliation
Months later
On another busy Saturday night
She had been drinking too much again
And after slights slipping out of the side of her mouth
I took the bait and answered back
A war of words commenced
But she took it to the next level
In her drunken stupor she decided to try and fight me
Mutual friends broke it up

But it was enough
I had lost yet another girlfriend I loved
Another sister gone
I remember my boss telling me they were going to fire her
I remember asking them to fire me instead
because she had a kid
He looked at me as if looking at a dog with a broken leg
I remember him saying
"If the roles were reversed, she would not do that for you"
I remember finally leaving that job and feeling the years speed up
I remember giving my life to music
I remember signing my first deal
I remember buying my first house
And I remember doing my first tour
I remember playing a sold-out show in Miami and having a fan
    wave a phone in the air and scream out
"IT'S MONICA! FROM BONGOS!"
I remember looking the other way
Swiftly
Because I've always been allergic to late love
And forgiving can still be forgiveness without having to feign a
smile
I remember working all night
And counting tips on the rooftop before the sun would rise
While the sky was still pink
I remember a lot

I still work until the morning
I still work on the weekends
And I still count my money twice
So in that respect
not much has changed
And I love that for me

27
STORAGE

Do you know what it is to be scared of going into your library
and finally deleting photos in your phone
that have long overstayed their welcome?

Not because of what you'll find
But because of what the photos will find in you

You fear that you will see their face
and not make it back out okay

You fear that you will turn to look too far back into a text
and break your neck

You fear that you will double tap their name
and reignite the flame
That always backfires
And ends up burning you

I pace
Then I walk to the mirror and I see a fragile face
And beg

"Jessie show yourself some grace
Just buy the extra iCloud space"

28
SOME NIGHTS

Some nights
I think the Beatles were wrong
Because some nights
All I need
is not love
I just need someone
who is down to polish off a bottle of Jameson
I just need someone
who doesn't make faces after we take shots
Someone who knows some of my favorite songs
And who likes to sing along
Someone that looks nothing like my type
Who knows that I've been ripe
And my fruit
Needs to
be eaten
slow
-ly
Someone who has also gotten used to being alone
So they don't get offended when I send them home
Some nights I don't need love
Some nights I just need a friend
Who knows how to get the job done
And doesn't judge me
When I tell them my heart is the only thing
that they're not allowed to touch

29
PRETTY

I asked you once if I looked pretty
And you smiled at me and said
"You are pretty as many times as God is good"
The corner of my lip curled up reluctantly
God is good
All the time

30
A TRYING FAILURE

I try and fail
I try to remember
how bored I'd feel sometimes
when you would submerge into your introverted silence
But I fail and end up remembering how in those muted moments
I could hear your heart
I remember watching the slightest pulse that your whole body
    would take on when you'd sleep
And you'd move on beat
I'd never seen that before
Considering how much love you held for me
it only makes sense that the smallest song in your chest
could make a whole man move in his sleep
as if dancing in slumber
as if God was rejoicing by having you closer in secret

I try and fail
I try and remember how much I used to wish you were more
    aggressive
I try and remember how my femininity longed to be dominated
But I fail
I fail and only remember how your kisses used to feel like petals
Petals falling on my skin
And how you used to melt into my embrace
after a long day
and say
how much you needed it
Needed me
Gently

I try and fail
I try and remember how much I longed for freedom
and how constrained hearing you speak of children would make me
    feel

I try and remember how it would make the veins on my neck tense
I try and remember how much I used to fear motherhood stealing
    my independence
How scared I was of motherhood rinsing me of my autonomy
and my beautiful youth
But I fail
I fail and feel my dreams of a child
born with your eyes and my smile
fade into a time
that will never be
I fail and instead remember a reality that will kill me if I live to see it
Where you hold another woman's hand as she gives you a son
Maybe a daughter
I fail and feel the years weighing down my skin
Made worse by the tears I've cried
As if they're eroding lines
down my face
every time that lying to myself goes left
And all I'm left with is the void
deep within a hole
Under a rock
Within my chest

Nonchalance looks like peace from a distance
Companionship looks like love from a distance
Rejection triggers attraction from a distance
And I'm so far off in the horizon now that
I don't even know if my thoughts are my own anymore
I'm lost in doubt
And being carried out farther by the current
Trying with everything I have to get out
But I keep failing
And so I try again

Because waiting in vain for your love
has only made nostalgia thicker
And has only made love songs hurt
And has only made me love you more

31
GRIP

Grip my heart
With fear of leaving
Make my stomach tense
Lure tears from my eyes
Please
Please
Because peaceful love has left me nothing but a suicide note
And fucked me the most with a gentle goodbye
Because only then
Once it finally got fed up of waiting for me to feel
Did I feel it grip
Only then did I fear I had really lost it
Only then did my senses wake
Only then did my stomach tense
Only then did it lure tears from my eyes
And years from my life
So to new love
Please
If you see the faintest of future in front of us
Please
Put the pain in front of me
On a sunny day
So that I may know what to cherish
Because unless it is painful
I cannot bear it
Unless I feel its nails in my skin
I am as blind to it as color is to a dog's eye
Help me be human
Help me in my sickness
And make it hurt
So I can feel

Please
Just a tinge of lover's pain
To verify it's real
Before love leaves me again

32
ALTRUISTIC

Before your eyes
And before the powdered sugar in the air around your being
Your altruism
was my favorite
Your kindness
is what I missed most
But in our final battle
God gave you the curse of a slip
And gave me the gift of sight
And finally removed my nostalgic cataracts
One night
Swollen eyes and sleepless bags were all I had to show for trying to
    save our "unconditional connection"
I was so outside of myself
Struggling with insecurities
Fighting visions of you and other women whom I could never be
And fighting my hardest to be better
Fighting to accept your need for space
Searching for atonement
For not having loved you on time
For having met you while my chest bled for another
But in my lowest moment
And in my heartbroken embarrassment
And in my mania of trying to get you to hear my words from miles
    away
Instead of kindness
Your eyes turned a deeper red than rose
And you showed me your thorns
And did to me
That which you condemned me for doing to you
And you showed me
A trait of your begetter
The reneged traits of your human design
And you vanished

Hypocrisy
is a burning hole
in the parachute of a former lover
who has fallen from a thousand-foot high pedestal
While the other stands and watches the fall

There
In the grass
Lies the dandelion-sized consolation of knowing they were never as
   great as you thought they were

You weren't as great as I thought you were
This whole time
you were just like them
But the quiet in your demeanor
lied and called itself kindness
And the fear in your perpetual reluctancy of confrontation
lied and called itself altruism

33
ACID WHISPER

Talking to you
is getting dangerous
For how easily you bring serenity to my feet
And how stark and dark the world becomes
when I am not what you're looking at

Talking to you is getting dangerous
For how quickly my Eden returns when I hear your voice
And how quickly hell dawns when I don't

Fear sneaks into my room as I am counting my skeletons
She pulls out a chair at the dinner table
And sits across from me
Sinisterly smiling
Waiting
While seconds hang in the air
Wet with the undeniable
Finally your name slides out of her curled lips like an acid whisper
Taunting
She sits there waiting for my thoughts to fizz outside of myself
Watching my body for the inevitable reaction
Watching my body respond to danger

Someone else walks in

Ego
Hello ego
Friend or foe?
I can't tell
She comes closer

"Lean in
I have a secret that fear cannot hear
I am at the gates of heaven again
I am at the gates of hell again
I am at the gates of love
Scared to death because
He is kind
He is joy
And he is peace
And I think his peace is eternal
With or without me
But mine only exists with him"

Fear shoots over a sharp glare at Ego
Ego whispers
"Act natural"

Suddenly the forces in the room violently collide
Like liquid magnets
Fear and Ego melt into each other
Until there is no one in the room
But me

My skeletons
And me

34
TIME

In my childhood
Most days would stand still
But that was only because I was watching the adults
Most of whom looked the same year after year
Who seemed to have no more growing to do
When I was born my aunt had gray hair
Today my aunt has gray hair
In my childhood
I bought the illusion of the finish line
I bought the illusion
of there being a group of humans
who carried the answer sheet I was looking for
But had I been looking next to me
I would've seen time's true nature
I would've seen the seasons speed up
I would've seen the years fly by
But like most children, only the summers ran past me
While September carried the width and weight of a fat warden
Ready to pull me back to jail
Back to school
Where my age and lack of autonomy
made the seconds move like molasses in reverse
Now in my adulthood
The warden is dead
And the years escape me like trying to stop a whole river with only
        my hands
And the years escape me like criminals running through a turnstile
        door at Alcatraz
And though adulthood demands some poise
Sometimes I just cry
And go against the tradition to lie to kids
When children look to me for a map
Because I myself don't even know where I stand

35
NIGHTMARE

Last night
was the first time
I ever had an internal monologue during a dream
In the dream
I was out with some acquaintances
The kind of acquaintances who love the nightlife
The kind who always wear red lipstick
The kind who used to steal as a children
I was out with them in the *Inception*-like streets of my dreamland
when I had a quintessential introverted moment
I asked myself
Why?
Why did I accept this invitation to come?
Why come if I never feel like myself at parties anyway?
Why was I willingly around people
Who make me feel
Like I have to second-guess everything I say
Before I even say it
People who make the voice in my head sound like an echo chamber
Echo
Chamber
Was the environment unsafe or was it personal insecurity?
I'm not sure
But
I was on edge
So I had to speak myself off the ledge
I took a deep breath
I told myself to make the most of it
And just when I was practicing Eckart Tolle's nonresistance
And just when I was feeling peace blossom in the deepest corner of
    my social anxiety–ridden bottled-up body
You walked through the door

With a smile and a half-empty bottle of Grey Goose in hand
And said "Oh the party's in here!"
Time slows down
My stomach churns
Your smile quickly turns to shock when you see me
And I roll my eyes and ask my friend
"Why?"
Then I woke up
Alone
But usually I wake up divided in two
Because there are two sides of me
The sickly optimistic subconscious side of me
Who used to summon you into my dreams
That side of me used to smile when she would see you
She used to hug you
She used to wake up sad from dreams
Because they were the only place that you would hug her back
She was at war with the strength in me
She was at war with the other me
The warrior in me
Who has wanted me healed
Who has waited years to see me at peace
Last night
The warrior must have finally won
And the lovesick version of me must've finally fallen
Because I woke up without you
And smiled

36
PROTECTION

"We should start using protection"
 I looked at you puzzled
"Think of your career" you said
 I always thought you were so supportive
 It took me years to see
 That you didn't want me to win
 You just knew I was your conduit
 And the depth of your darkness
 And the depth of your selfishness
 was hiding
 beneath a seven-year age difference
 that you took full advantage of
 I believed you
 When you told me I was crazy
 for going through your phone and catching you in another lie
 I believed you
 when you told me I was crazy
 For thinking your drinking was a problem
 I believed you
 when you told me
"We should start using protection"
 For the sake of my career
 And we did
 For weeks
 Until that one night in Chicago
 When you were swimming in rum
 And we went skin to skin
 Like we used to
 And you paused for a moment
 Like a thief listening for a creak in the home they've broken into
 Then you continued
 My intuition was deep asleep
 And deafened by denial

It took me months to wake up to undeniable evidence
And finally vindicate the harbingers I had ignored
Like echoes from the past
"We should start using protection" hit my ears
like the glow of red walking into the room
Before the devil does
To offer his fruits
And I was so starved for love
That I didn't notice the mold

37
DAYS

We used to square up in the early days
But then with time
My self-worth withered
So I wouldn't argue back
I would just let you scream
And I would cry
And I would beg you to stay
And I would sit by the edge of the window
Ten stories up
Because at the time
I would rather have died
Than watch you walk away
I was sick
I was broken
I hated the mirror
But I still loved you
You would wake up the next day hungover
But closer to sober
And we would try to mend it
And we'd be okay
For a sweet second
The kind of second that melts in your mouth before you can actually
    taste it
Then the bitter cycle would start again
But I couldn't fault you
Because you were just a bottle of anger and male aggression
With family trauma
And shitty friends
And any other possible scapegoat excuse I could muster up
Just to absolve you of any responsibility
It was just "who you were"

One day
While out without me
You came face to face
with the man who had told me to kneel and open wide
if I ever wanted my dreams to come to life
And dangled my future in front of me
You came face to face with my gatekeeper
And you kept it from me
Until days later
You finally let it slip
And it stumbled off of your lips
In passing
And then you jumped to another topic like a frog
As if it wouldn't shake me
Your train of thought continued as if nothing
As if my body wasn't on the rails
"Wait. What did you do when you met him?" I asked
"What do you mean?" you answered

I paused while my thoughts floated back in time
To our early days
It was our second date
Somewhere by the lake
Where I had told you the details
And you had said that you "wish you could've been there"
So you could've "protected" me
Yet another fallacy
That I believed
Because now that fate had dealt you the moment
And you were face to face
With a certified enemy
You did nothing

"What did you do when you met him?" I asked again
"Nothing"
You answered
I thought to myself in that moment
He can scream bloody murder
at me
He can put on a violent show and hurl curses
at me
He can bring his fists to the walls with fury in my name and scream
  his anger
at me
But not for me
You were never for me

38
ATOMS

Adam and Eve
Atom and EVErything

An ode
To all that was here before me and that which will remain after

To my beautiful great aunt Mercedes
Who cried with me as the taxi took off to the airport the last time I
    saw her
She had skin the color of oak
And she had as much love as a tree does for the ground it comes
    from
Except she had it for everyone

To my kind uncle Marcelino
Who I never saw angry
Not even once
He had a voice that would comfort even a stranger's soul
Like a wool blanket in an Algonquin cabin in December
And he only spoke words that did his timbre justice

To my tender childhood friend Andrew
Whose smile was as contagious as a domino fall
He had a kind innocence
that made you feel as though
you were witnessing an angel's first time on earth
And he would befriend even a rabid dog in spite of the risk
Because he couldn't help but see the good in everyone

To my vibrant aunt Amparo
Who had a heart so big it barely fit in her chest
She painted works of art that would make you question if you had
ever seen that color before
And she would have cooked love-filled meals for everyone she'd ever
met if she could've
Because the warmth of her motherhood was indiscriminate

Many of my loved ones exist as atoms now
And sit in the world of spirit
Where I believe we'll all go after we graduate
from this torpid realm we live in
And at the risk of sounding morbid
Some nights when I miss their smiles
I just can't wait to die

39
STUCK

If I live to see the day
That I lose my deepest love
Any pain I've ever felt
Will have been a walk in the park
Because I know
That hell
Is earth
Without them
And I know
That breath
Will feel like a curse
Without them
And if heaven doesn't accept those
That plunge themselves into the afterlife
I know I'll be stuck here
Without them
Just waiting
Just begging
For God to take my years away
So forgive me
If I stand on the edge of a building
And beg the world to shake

40
ICARUS

I still lived in the west
My room was a mess
And my ghetto single mattress was on the floor
Adorned with his naked body
Somehow he still looked like a king
I was in the shower
Bathing in holy water
Staring at the wall in disbelief
And flying high in euphoria
Because it was the first time
in years
that I felt what I was feeling
It was love
The all-encompassing kind
And I couldn't wipe off the smile
But then I thought of Icarus
And how we share a trait
And I felt a sudden fear in my gut
Because I remembered
I've never fallen gracefully
And in that moment
You were my sun
I was millions of feet from the ground
And at this impossible height
My wings were bound to burn
And I knew it

41
INDIFFERENCE

I wear indifference like a fur coat in the arctic
But I am barefoot

I take deep breaths
And force the drums in my chest to drop

You are the northern winds that burn my face
But I am peace

I am peace in spite of you

I am peace in spite of you

Until my breath gives my truth away in the air

And small clouds of the past escape from my lips

And memories of you dance in front of my face

I realize
It's not cold here
in my heart
You just can't feel the warmth from the outside
But you can see it
Like the sun in December

42
VIDA

Ojalá mi vida termine antes que la tuya
Porque si fueras a morir primero
te seguiría por la puerta
En cambio tú
Siempre tienes una fuerza de oro que te decora
Y incluso si me voy
Sé que todavía encontrarás la luz
Porque sos la luz
Y tu sol seguirá saliendo al amanecer
Porque sos el sol
No es justo
Pero es la única forma
Que al menos uno de nosotros
Llegue a ver otro día
Necesito que me prometas que me dejarás ir
y aprenderás a sonreír sin mí.
Y bailarás hasta que estén toditos tus pelos blanquitos
A pesar de las lágrimas en tus ojos
Necesito que me prometas
Que vas a estar aquí
cuando yo me vaya
Porque yo sé
que yo no sobreviviré
tus despedidas
Y si vivo para ver tu tumba
Sabré que la mía no se queda atrás
Sos mi suspiro
Sos los colores en mi mañana
Mi redención
Y mi oración
Y la vida simplemente no puede ser vida
Si no estas aquí

43
A GOAT

To you
My unknown life support
Without you
I am nothing
Without you
My painting has no frame
Without you
My wick has no flame
Without you
My name has no claim to fame
Without you
My parents would still be afraid
Afraid of a child who just floats
Afraid of a child who just roams the world without purpose
And though art has always been my home
Without you
My home would have no heat
So as a gift
To those who have made the bricks that have built my life
I give you the gift
that has changed mine
The power of the tongue
And the power of the word
That is of profound worth
When uttered daily
Regardless of conviction
Because I have learned
That repetition is what holds the elixir
So I give you a goat
An offering
A talisman
A wish list
A future unmanifested

And the proposition
Of practicing this beautiful magic
Together
Fill in the spaces
Build your castle
Paint your masterpiece
Mend your heart
And ascend to where you belong
Because we are children of expression
And we are here to blossom

I AM_____

I AM_____

I AM_____

I AM_____

I AM_____

× 5
Once a day for twenty-one days
With just a sprinkle of faith
For you and I are the same
And this is how my blessings came
I hope this helps
I hope this message finds you well

And in the event that you feel stuck
I hope this letter shifts your luck
With love
And infinite gratitude
—Jessie

AFFIRMATIONS FOR #43

AT PEACE
STRONG
BEAUTIFUL
SUCCESSFUL
UPLIFTING TO MYSELF
   AND OTHERS
A MOGUL
A GREAT ARTIST
LOVING
HAPPY
DISCIPLINED

DETERMINED
ENTHUSIASTIC
LEADING MY FIELD
TALENTED
HEALTHY
FORGIVING
KIND
CONNECTED
ACHIEVING MY FULL
   POTENTIAL
GRATEFUL FOR MY LIFE

Acknowledgments

Thank you to God. Thank you to my mom and dad for everything. To my therapist. To my seventh-grade English teacher Mrs. Hidden, who was the only teacher to ever call my house with good news after she saw that I had found a home in writing.

Thank you to my teams at FMLY, WME, Andrews McMeel, Simon & Schuster, and HarperCollins Publishing. Thank you to Haley Heidemann, Angeline Rodriguez, Brad Wilson, and Zach Iser. My dog. Special thank you to my editor, Danys Mares, for being so helpful and for holding space.

And lastly, thank you to my motherfucking self.

About the Author

Written by Gavin Sheppard

Jessie Reyez burns bright.

Serving as a light in the dark for a legion of loyal fans, Jessie channels her lived experiences and remarkable empathy into cathartic artistry. Celebrated as a songwriter, recording artist, live performer, philanthropist, activist, and author, Jessie is cementing her status as a storyteller across mediums.

Jessie Reyez was born in Toronto, Canada, to Colombian immigrants and raised between worlds. Linguistically and culturally fluid, Jessie has always had music as a universal grounding point. Taught guitar by her father at a young age, Jessie would explore various means of expression from instruments to voice to dance; poetry, however, was always her first love. Whether performing on festival stages, speaking in intimate interviews, or gracing live television, Jessie connects deeply with her words. A prolific writer, she captures the human experience in a way that is at once unique and relatable. Her sparks turn to wildfires that burn down decay and make space for beauty to bloom again. Outside of her own songs, she has lent her talents to others, penning records for the likes of Calvin Harris, Dua Lipa, Sam Smith, and Kehlani.

Today, Jessie has already enjoyed a storied career as a recording artist. After releasing critically acclaimed EPs (*Kiddo* and *Being Human in Public)* and albums (*Before Love Came to Kill Us* and *YESSIE*) that have accumulated over three billion streams, the Grammy-nominated, multiple Juno Award–winning, multiplatinum selling, Billboard Women in Music Impact Award recipient, MTV Video Music Award–nominated phenom is stepping back from the microphone and out of her comfort zone, starting again at the bottom of a new profession.

A hopeful romantic with a history of heartbreak, Jessie cuts deep to the bone with her writing and bares raw emotion. *Words of a Goat Princess* is not a blueprint in how to get over a broken heart, but rather an extension of Jessie's ongoing dialogue with the self and her latest attempt to reconcile idealism and experience.

Jessie is a global citizen, and her words have resounded across every continent on the map. Jessie's days alternating between touring and escaping have allowed her to soak up the human condition in all of its joy, misery, excitement, and banality. Her prized possessions are her memories and her most precious moments are with her family.

Jessie Reyez currently splits her time between Toronto, Canada, and Los Angeles, California.

About the Illustrator

Braktosaure (Eloïse Diot), a French Caribbean illustrator from Guadeloupe, thrives in capturing moods through her unique and evocative artwork.

With a style that blends darkness and naivety, she translates raw emotions through touching characters, inviting viewers to embark on a journey of self-reflection.

Her art features imperfect lines and a special affinity for black and white, adding to the emotional resonance.

You may recognize her work from her contributions to the artwork on Jessie Reyez's critically acclaimed project "Being Human in Public."

Immersing oneself in Braktosaure's universe calls for a cathartic introspection within the beautifully melancholic world she creates.